LITHUANIA 2016 HUMAN RIGHTS REPORT

EXECUTIVE SUMMARY

The Republic of Lithuania is a constitutional, multiparty, parliamentary democracy. Legislative authority resides in a unicameral parliament (Seimas), and executive authority resides in the Office of the President. Observers evaluated the 2014 presidential elections and parliamentary elections on October 9 and 23 as generally free and fair.

Civilian authorities maintained effective control over the security forces.

The most serious human rights problems concerned aspects of the justice system, children's welfare, and intolerance toward minorities. In the justice system, conditions were substandard in a number of prison and detention facilities, and lengthy pretrial detention remained a problem. Children experienced abuse, both in families and in institutions, which increased exposure to delinquency, trafficking, and prostitution. Intolerance took the form of xenophobia, anti-Semitism, prejudice against ethnic minorities and against lesbian, gay, bisexual, transgender, and intersex (LGBTI) persons; Roma continued to experience poor living conditions often in areas of high crime, and faced social exclusion and discrimination.

Additional problems included "antipropaganda" laws restricting freedom of speech and expression, authorities' refusal to grant asylum interviews to persons deemed to have arrived from "safe" countries of origin or transit, and isolated reports of government corruption. Laws against spousal rape were inadequate, and domestic violence was widespread. There was a culture of silence around sexual harassment. Trafficking in persons remained a problem, as did social integration and inadequate access to services and facilities for persons with disabilities.

The government took measures to prosecute or otherwise punish officials who committed abuses, whether in the security services or elsewhere.

Section 1. Respect for the Integrity of the Person, Including Freedom from:

a. Arbitrary Deprivation of Life and other Unlawful or Politically Motivated Killings

There were no reports that the government or its agents committed arbitrary or unlawful killings.

b. Disappearance

There were no reports of politically motivated disappearances.

c. Torture and Other Cruel, Inhuman, or Degrading Treatment or Punishment

The constitution and law prohibit such practices, and there were no reports that government officials employed them.

Prison and Detention Center Conditions

Some prison and detention center conditions did not meet international standards.

<u>Physical Conditions</u>: Four prison inmates died during the first eight months of the year, three by suicide and one from disease. Authorities initiated four pretrial investigations but found no evidence of criminal wrongdoing. Prisoners complained of poor hygiene in rooms for visitors and other premises, inadequate medical care, poor food, substandard sanitary conditions, limited supplies of personal hygiene products, and limited hour of operation of shops located in prisons.

In its 2014 report, the Council of Europe's Committee for the Prevention of Torture (CPT) noted that access to natural light in most detention facilities and prisons was inadequate, and in-cell toilets were partitioned only partly or not at all. The report found that mattresses and blankets were often filthy and worn out, particularly at the Joniskis and Kelme police facilities.

<u>Administration</u>: Authorities generally investigated credible allegations of inhuman conditions. Although no ombudsman was specifically dedicated to prison matters, a section of the Office of the Parliamentary Ombudsman specifically investigated prisoner complaints and attempted to resolve them, usually by making recommendations to the directors of the institutions concerned. The ombudsman's office reported that institutions were responsive to all of its interventions. The ombudsman's office found eight of the 32 complaints it investigated by September 1, to be justified. The parliamentary ombudsman visited detention facilities and detainees on a regular basis. During such visits, he evaluated conditions and

treatment of detainees as well as the implementation of CPT recommendations and of the UN Optional Protocol against Torture and other Cruel, Inhuman or Degrading Treatment or Punishment (OPCAT), and prepared written reports for authorities with recommendations.

Independent Monitoring: The government permitted monitoring by independent nongovernmental observers. On September 5-15, the CPT conducted a periodic visit to the country.

Improvements: Between January and September, the government spent approximately 364,000 euros ($400,000) on the renovation of seven prison facilities. The improvements included renovations of housing, medical units, and food service facilities in prisons at Marijampole, Alytus, and Vilnius, and the establishment of a safe house in Panevezys for mothers with young children and of a secondary school at the Kaunas juvenile detention facility.

d. Arbitrary Arrest or Detention

The law prohibits arbitrary arrest and detention, and the government generally observed these prohibitions.

Role of the Police and Security Apparatus

The principal responsibility of the State Security Department is to identify activities that pose a threat to the security of the state, its territorial inviolability and integrity, its interests, and its economic and defense potential. It reported to parliament. Police and the State Border Guards Service were subordinate to the Ministry of Interior. Military forces were under the Ministry of Defense. The Special Investigative Service, the main anticorruption agency, reported to the president and the parliament. Civilian authorities maintained effective control over the security forces. The government had effective mechanisms to investigate and punish abuse and corruption. There were no reports of impunity involving the security forces.

Arrest Procedures and Treatment of Detainees

Except for persons arrested during the commission of a crime, warrants are generally required for arrests, and judges may issue them only upon the presentation of reliable evidence of criminal activity. Police may detain suspects for up to 48 hours before formally charging them. Detainees have the right to be informed of the charges against them at the time of their arrest or their first interrogation, and there were no complaints of failure to comply with this requirement.

Bail was available and widely used. The law provides for access to an attorney, and the state provided one to indigent persons. In its 2014 report, the CPT noted that while most of the detainees interviewed claimed they had legal counsel at the first investigative interview, it appeared that police rarely granted access to an attorney at earlier stages of police custody. Some detainees who had appointed attorneys complained that they met their attorney for the first time at the court hearing, even in instances when they requested an attorney shortly after their arrest. Detainees had prompt access to family members.

Pretrial Detention: The law permits authorities to hold suspects under house arrest for up to six months, a period that a judge may extend at his discretion. A pretrial judge may order that a suspect facing felony charges be detained for up to three months, but only to prevent the accused from fleeing, committing new crimes, or hindering the investigation; or to comply with extradition requests. In many cases the law permits detention to be extended to 18 months (six months for juveniles), subject to appeal to a higher court. Judges frequently granted such extensions, often based on the allegation that the defendant would pose a danger to society or influence witnesses. The maximum period authorities could detain a person charged with minor offenses is nine months and for juveniles six months.

In the first half of the year, the average length of pretrial detention was approximately 11 months. As of September 1, approximately 58 percent of incarcerated persons were pretrial detainees. The law allows defense attorneys access to the evidence prosecutors use to justify pretrial detention.

Detainee's Ability to Challenge Lawfulness of Detention before a Court: The constitution provides the right to challenge the validity of a detention before a court and subsequent compensation for any damages resulting from the unlawful deprivation of liberty. Authorities respected this right.

e. Denial of Fair Public Trial

The constitution provides for an independent judiciary, and the government generally respected judicial independence.

Trial Procedures

The constitution and law provide the right to a fair public trial, and an independent judiciary generally enforced this right.

Defendants have a right to a presumption of innocence, prompt and detailed information about the charges against them, a fair and public trial without undue delay and to be present at their trial. Defendants have a right to communicate with an attorney of their choice (or have one provided at public expense), adequate time and facilities to prepare a defense, free interpretation as necessary from the moment charged through all appeals, and access to government-held evidence. They are entitled to confront witnesses against them, to present witnesses and evidence in their defense, and to be free of compulsion to testify or confess guilt. They enjoy the right of appeal. Authorities usually respected these rights and extended them to all defendants.

Political Prisoners and Detainees

There were no reports of political prisoners or detainees.

Civil Judicial Procedures and Remedies

There is an independent and impartial judiciary in civil matters. Plaintiffs may sue for legal relief or temporary protection measures from human rights violations. Persons alleging human rights abuses may also appeal to the parliamentary ombudsman for a determination of the merits of their claims. Although the ombudsman has the authority only to make recommendations to an offending institution, such institutions generally honored the ombudsman's recommendations. Individuals alleging that the state had violated the European Convention on Human Rights could, after exhausting domestic legal remedies, appeal to the European Court of Human Rights.

Property Restitution

A philanthropic foundation created in 2011 to receive government compensation for Communist and Nazi seizures of Jewish community-owned property distributed funds to individuals and to Jewish educational, cultural, scientific, and religious projects. According to an agreement between the government and the Jewish community, the foundation was to disburse the equivalent of 128 million litas (then the national currency--approximately $49 million) over a 10-year period, beginning in 2012. The foundation distributed a one-time payment of three million litas (approximately $950,000) to individual survivors in 2013 and 2014. The remaining funds were allocated to support Jewish educational, cultural, scientific, and religious projects, as decided by the foundation board. During the year the foundation received 3.62 million euros ($3.98 million) which brought the total received since 2011 to 14.48 million euros ($15.9 million). Jewish and ethnic Polish communities continued to advocate for private property restitution, since there had been no opportunity to submit individual claims since 2001.

f. Arbitrary or Unlawful Interference with Privacy, Family, Home, or Correspondence

The constitution prohibits such actions, but there were reports that the government did not respect this prohibition.

The law requires authorities to obtain a judge's authorization before searching an individual's premises. It prohibits indiscriminate monitoring, including e-mail, text messages, or other digital communications intended to remain private. Domestic human rights groups alleged that the government did not properly enforce the law. In the first six months of the year, the State Data Protection Inspectorate investigated 189 allegations of privacy violations, compared with 262 such allegations in the first eight months of 2015. Most complaints involved claims by individuals that their personal information, such as identity numbers, was collected without a legal justification. Most claims were against private companies, but there were some complaints against the government. During the first six months of the year, the inspectorate conducted 11 preventive, as opposed to complaint-driven, investigations of enterprises and government agencies for possible violations, compared with 60 such audits in the first eight months of 2015.

Section 2. Respect for Civil Liberties, Including:

a. Freedom of Speech and Press

The constitution provides for freedom of speech and press, although the law prohibits "hate speech" and dissemination of certain other objectionable materials, such as war propaganda, calls for violently changing the constitutional order, or challenges to the country's sovereignty or territorial integrity. The government generally respected these rights. An independent press, an effective judiciary, and a functioning democratic political system combined to promote freedom of speech and press.

<u>Freedom of Speech and Expression</u>: The constitutional definition of freedom of expression does not include slander; disinformation; or incitement to violence, discrimination, or national, racial, religious, or social hatred. Inciting hatred against a group of persons is punishable by imprisonment for up to two years. Inciting violence against a group of persons is punishable by imprisonment for up to three years.

It is a crime to deny or "grossly to trivialize" Soviet or Nazi German crimes against the country or its citizens, or to deny genocide, crimes against humanity, or war crimes.

On April 14, parliament passed a law criminalizing the disclosure or publication of information heard during a closed court session. Violations may be punished by community service, fine, imprisonment, or arrest. Media professionals criticized the law, saying it threatened freedom of expression and contradicted the rights and protections for journalists established by Lithuanian courts and the European Court of Human Rights.

In the first eight months of the year, according to the Ministry of Interior, authorities initiated investigations into 24 allegations of incitement of hatred, mostly involving the internet. In the same period investigators forwarded 27 incitement cases (some from previous years) to the courts for trial and closed 24 for lack of evidence. A number of other investigations continued. Most such allegations involved racist or anti-Semitic expression or hostility based on sexual orientation, gender identity, or nationality.

<u>Press and Media Freedoms</u>: Independent media were active and expressed a wide variety of views. They were subject to the same laws that prohibit hate speech and criminalize speech that grossly trivializes international and war crimes.

<u>Censorship or Content Restrictions</u>: In June the Lithuanian Radio and Television Commission cancelled restrictions on two Russian-language television channels imposed in 2015 after signals from the European Commission that the sanctions might run counter to EU legislation. In November the Radio and Television Commission suspended one of the channels again for three months on the charge of inciting war, discord, and hatred towards nations.

The law makes insulting or defaming the president of the country in the mass media a crime punishable by a fine. Authorities did not invoke it during the year.

It is illegal to publish material that is "detrimental to minors' bodies" or thought processes or that promotes the sexual abuse and harassment of minors, sexual relations among minors, or "sexual relations." Human rights observers continued to criticize this law (see section 6, Acts of Violence, Discrimination, and Other Abuses Based on Sexual Orientation and Gender Identity). LGBTI groups claimed that it served as a rationale for limiting LGBTI awareness-raising efforts and that agencies overseeing publishing and broadcast media took prejudicial action against the coverage of stories with LGBTI themes.

Internet Freedom

The government did not restrict or disrupt access to the internet or censor online content, and there were no credible reports that the government monitored private online communications without appropriate legal authority. Authorities investigated and prosecuted internet speech considered to incite hatred. For example, on August 8, prosecutors opened an investigation into antigay comments published online following the attack on the Orlando, Florida, nightclub. On September 9, an appeals court acquitted a comedian convicted in 2015 for inciting hatred and violence against children after posting a video clip called "Satan, I ask" on YouTube.

According to the Information Society Development Committee under the Ministry of Transportation, 72 percent of the population regularly used the internet during the year.

Academic Freedom and Cultural Events

There were no government restrictions on academic freedom or cultural events.

b. Freedom of Peaceful Assembly and Association

Freedom of Assembly

The law and constitution provide for freedom of assembly, and the government generally respected this right.

Freedom of Association

Although the law provides for this freedom and the government generally respected it, the government continued to ban the Communist Party and other organizations associated with the Soviet period.

c. Freedom of Religion

See the Department of State's *International Religious Freedom Report* at www.state.gov/religiousfreedomreport/.

d. Freedom of Movement, Internally Displaced Persons, Protection of Refugees, and Stateless Persons

The constitution and law provide for freedom of internal movement, foreign travel, emigration, and repatriation, and the government generally respected these rights.

The government cooperated with the Office of the UN High Commissioner for Refugees and other humanitarian organizations in providing protection and assistance to refugees, returning refugees, asylum seekers, stateless persons, and other persons of concern.

Protection of Refugees

Access to Asylum: The law provides for the granting of asylum or refugee status, and the government has established a system for providing protection to refugees.

Safe Country of Origin/Transit: As a matter of policy, authorities barred asylum seekers coming from "safe" countries of transit and returned them to such countries without reviewing the substantive merits of their applications. During the first half of the year, the Migration Department denied 49 requests for asylum. The government's participation in the EU's effort to address high levels of migration into Europe was an exception to this policy.

Durable Solutions: The country began accepting foreigners under the EU's refugee resettlement program. By October 19, the country had admitted 172 refugees; as of November, however, 32 of these had left the country for other EU states. In December 2015 the Ministry of Social Affairs and Labor reduced financial support to asylum seekers and refugees by up to 50 percent following their first six months of residence. Nongovernmental organizations (NGOs) and independent experts criticized this policy, asserting that refugees require full support for longer than six months and would be at risk for poverty and homelessness. In July the minister of the interior criticized the conditions surrounding the refugee reception center at Rukla, claiming they were insufficient to support integration of refugees into Lithuanian society.

Temporary Protection: The government could grant "temporary protection" to groups of persons, not individuals, in the event of a mass influx of foreigners. Authorities could also grant "subsidiary protection" to individuals who may not qualify as refugees, and during the first half of the year provided it to six persons.

Stateless Persons

According to the Migration Department, 3,645 persons, or approximately 9 percent of all foreign residents in 2015 were stateless. The law permits persons born on the territory or legally residing there for 10 years, who are not citizens of any other country, to apply for citizenship. Applicants must possess an unlimited residence permit, knowledge of the Lithuanian language and constitution, and the ability to support themselves.

There was a modest decline in statelessness, due primarily to high emigration rates driven more by economic imperatives than naturalization considerations; only a few hundred persons obtained citizenship each year. Most persons classified as stateless were residents of the country at the time of the dissolution of the Soviet Union who did not take advantage of their right to qualify for citizenship. The total also included persons who, as part of the naturalization process, were temporarily "stateless" after relinquishing their former nationality but before acquiring that of Lithuania.

Section 3. Freedom to Participate in the Political Process

The constitution provides citizens the ability to choose their government in free and fair periodic elections held by secret ballot and based on universal and equal suffrage.

Elections and Political Participation

Recent Elections: Presidential elections, including a runoff between the top two candidates, took place in 2014. Parliamentary elections took place on October 9 and 23. Observers evaluated these elections as generally free and fair.

<u>Political Parties and Political Participation</u>: The government continued to prohibit the Communist Party.

<u>Participation of Women and Minorities</u>: No laws limit the participation of women and members of minorities in the political process, and women and minorities did participate.

Section 4. Corruption and Lack of Transparency in Government

The law provides criminal penalties for corruption by officials, but the government did not implement the law effectively. Officials at times engaged in corrupt practices with impunity. There were isolated reports of government corruption during the year.

<u>Corruption</u>: A corruption probe in May toppled the leadership of the Liberal Party after media reported a legal investigation of party leader Eligijus Masiulis for accepting a bribe of 100,000 euros ($110,000) from a prominent Lithuanian holding company, MG Baltic. On May 20, Masiulis resigned his parliamentary seat while the investigation continued.

NGOs, such as the domestic chapter of Transparency International (TI), considered health-sector corruption, including at state-supported institutions, a pervasive problem. A recent TI study described shortcomings in the transparency of defense procurement. It also noted that most of the charity and support foundations linked to members of parliament did not provide public information about their activities.

<u>Financial Disclosure</u>: The law requires appointed and elected officials to declare their assets and incomes. The declarations were available to the public. There were administrative sanctions for noncompliance. During the year the Chief Ethics Commission found that Minister of Culture Sarunas Birutis improperly declared his partial ownership of a business interest in Bulgaria.

<u>Public Access to Information</u>: The law provides for public access to government information, and government institutions generally provided access. Applicants could appeal denials to the parliamentary ombudsman. In the first eight months of the year, the Office of the Parliamentary Ombudsman received 42 complaints of delays by government offices in providing information. In the same period, it ruled on 23 cases, found 11 to be valid, and recommended disciplinary action against the officials involved. The ombudsman's office rejected 23 complaints as not being within its competence and referred them to the agencies with jurisdiction.

Although the ombudsman's recommendations were not binding, the office reported that authorities took disciplinary action in all cases.

Section 5. Governmental Attitude Regarding International and Nongovernmental Investigation of Alleged Violations of Human Rights

A number of domestic and international human rights groups generally operated without government restriction, investigating and publishing their findings on human rights cases. Government officials were generally cooperative and responsive to their views.

Government Human Rights Bodies: The equal opportunities ombudsman heads an independent public institution with responsibility for implementing and enforcing rights under the Law of Equal Treatment and for investigating individual complaints. A children's rights ombudsman has responsibility for overseeing observance of children's rights and their legal interests and can initiate investigations of possible violations of such rights, either upon receipt of a complaint or on its own initiative. The parliamentary ombudsman investigated complaints about abuse of office or other violations of human rights and freedoms involving public administration and implemented the national prevention of torture mechanism under the OPCAT. Some human rights observers questioned the effectiveness of all the ombudsman institutions.

Parliament's human rights committee prepares and reviews draft laws and other legal acts related to civil rights and presents recommendations to state institutions and other organizations about problems related to the protection of civil rights. It also receives reports from the Office of the Parliamentary Ombudsman.

Section 6. Discrimination, Societal Abuses, and Trafficking in Persons

Women

Rape and Domestic Violence: Rape and domestic violence are criminal offenses. Penalties for domestic violence depend on the level of injury to the victim, ranging from required public service to life imprisonment. In the first eight months of the year, authorities received 74 reports of rape, compared with 122 during the same period in 2015. Convicted rapists generally received prison sentences of three to five years. NGOs reported that sexual violence against women, including from intimate partners, remained a problem. No law specifically criminalizes spousal rape, and no data on spousal rape was available.

The penalties for domestic violence depend on the level of injury inflicted on the victim. The law permits rapid government action in domestic violence cases. For example, police and other law enforcement officials may, with court approval, require perpetrators to live apart from their victims, avoid all contact with them, and surrender any weapons they may possess.

Domestic violence remained a pervasive problem. The NGO Human Rights Monitoring Group contended that one in three women suffered from physical, psychological, or sexual abuse. In the first eight months of the year, police received 33,453 domestic violence calls and started 6,718 pretrial investigations, including 24 for murder.

Municipal governments and NGOs funded and operated 20 specialized regional help centers for victims of domestic violence. The national government fully funded two others. One of the latter, the Shelter for Children and Mothers, located in Vilnius, assisted more than 100 victims of domestic violence and human trafficking during the year.

During the year the Ministry of Social Security and Labor increased assistance for victims of domestic violence, allocating 670,000 euros ($737,000), compared with 266,000 euros ($292,600) in 2015. The ministry selected six NGOs to provide specialized assistance to victims of domestic violence. These organizations assisted more than 8,000 such victims in 2015.

Sexual Harassment: The law prohibits sexual harassment, but women who experienced it remained reluctant to approach police or other institutions because of lack of confidence that authorities would respond and because of the perceived stigma associated with making such matters public. In the first eight months of the year, the equal opportunities ombudsman received no complaints of sexual harassment. On June 7, parliament passed an amendment to the Law on Equal Opportunities for Women and Men banning gender-based harassment. Under this law employers are responsible for ensuring that employees are not subjected to gender-based harassment and sexual harassment at work.

Reproductive Rights: The government recognized the basic right of couples and individuals to decide the number, spacing, and timing of their children; manage their reproductive health; and have the information and means to do so, free from discrimination, coercion and violence.

<u>Discrimination</u>: Men and women have the same legal status and rights. Women nevertheless continued to face discrimination. The law requires equal pay for equal work, but women often earned less than their male counterparts.

Children

<u>Birth Registration</u>: Citizenship can be acquired either by birth in the country or from one's parents. The government registered all births promptly.

<u>Child Abuse</u>: NGOs noted that, despite a multi-year effort to combat violence against children, many problems continued. In 2015 according to the latest information from the Department of Statistics, 19,043 children lived in 9,757 "at-risk" families, including those experiencing substance abuse, unemployment, and other socioeconomic problems. Media frequently reported instances of cruelty to children, including sexual abuse, intentional starvation, and beating. The Department of Statistics registered 1,669 reports of violence against children in 2015. The children's rights ombudsman reported receiving 154 complaints in the first eight months of the year.

The ombudsman for children's rights reported that government efforts to combat child abuse and aid abused children were ineffective. In the first eight months of the year, Child Line (a hotline for children and youth) received 421,697 telephone calls from children but, because of limited human and financial resources, it could respond only to 192 calls. Child Line also answered 883 letters from children, whose concerns ranged from relations with their parents and friends to family violence and sexual abuse.

Sexual abuse of children remained a problem despite prison sentences of up to 13 years for the crime. In the first eight months of the year, the Ministry of Interior recorded 33 cases of child rape and 98 cases involving other forms of child sexual abuse. The government operated a children's support center to provide special care for children who suffered from violence, including sexual violence. On June 3, the minister of social security and labor opened a center in Vilnius to provide legal, psychological, and medical assistance to sexually abused children and their families.

<u>Early and Forced Marriage</u>: The minimum age for marriages for girls and boys is 18.

<u>Sexual Exploitation of Children</u>: Individuals involving a child in pornographic events or using a child in the production of pornographic material are subject to imprisonment for up to five years. During the same period, the Office of the Ombudsman for Children's Rights reported that it received one complaint and initiated one investigation of sexual exploitation of children. No information was available about the number of persons convicted of sexually exploiting children. According to the Ministry of Interior, officials opened five criminal cases involving child pornography during the first eight months of the year. The age of consent is 16.

<u>Displaced Children</u>: Street children were widely scattered among the country's cities. Most were runaways or from dysfunctional families. According to the Missing Persons Families Support Center, 3,241 persons, including 2,048 children, were reported missing in 2015.

A number of free, government-sponsored programs assisted displaced children. Government bodies and numerous NGOs administered 60 agencies protecting children's rights to aid vulnerable children.

<u>Institutionalized Children</u>: In 2015, 3,868 orphans and other children in need of care resided in the country's 95 orphanages, including 17 operated by NGOs and 52 large-family foster homes. There were five boarding schools for children with disabilities. As of September 1, the children's rights ombudsman received three complaints and started one investigation regarding children's rights violations in these institutions. Under the law children under the age of three are sent to guardianship institutions only in exceptional cases when they need specialized health care, nursing, or when the family or municipality cannot provide a child with proper care. To speed up the adoption process, the law also limits a child's stay in an orphanage to 12 months as opposed to the longstanding pattern of temporary care in orphanages lasting five years or longer, representing one of the main obstacles to children's adoption by new families.

NGOs, child welfare experts, and psychologists contended that the country's orphanages were detrimental to child development, leading to a wide range of social problems, such as delinquency, social exclusion, and vulnerability to trafficking and prostitution. In March 2015 prosecutors announced an investigation into allegations that the director of the Viesvile Orphanage sexually exploited boys in his care. These allegations followed a January announcement that prosecutors were investigating the Sveksna School--a residential institution for children with special needs--for hosting a prostitution ring in which 15- to 17-year-old residents prostituted younger female residents. The director was dismissed during the pretrial investigation, which continued at year's end.

International Child Abductions: The country is not a party to the 1980 Hague Convention on the Civil Aspects of International Child Abduction. See the Department of State's *Annual Report on International Parental Child Abduction* at travel.state.gov/content/childabduction/en/legal/compliance.html.

Anti-Semitism

The Jewish community consisted of approximately 4,000 persons. There were reports of anti-Semitic acts and vandalism throughout the year. For example, on April 28, a window of the Lithuanian Jewish community center was broken. On May 2, police opened a pretrial investigation into the incident.

Anti-Semitic expression was especially evident on the internet.

Police had instructions to take preemptive measures against illegal activities, giving special attention to maintaining order on specific historical dates and certain religious or cultural holidays.

On February 16, the Lithuanian Nationalist Union held its annual march in Kaunas. Media estimated that 250-300 participants marched, fewer than in 2015. Police were present to monitor the event, and there were no reports of violence. As in past years, participants chanted the slogan "Lithuania for Lithuanians." Some groups, including the Simon Wiesenthal Center, observed the march and reported the presence of Nazi-like symbols.

On May 5, the March of the Living took place at the Paneriai Memorial in Vilnius. The march retraced the route of residents of the Vilnius ghetto to the massacre awaiting them in the Paneriai Forest.

On June 6, President Dalia Grybauskaite signed into law amendments to the country's citizenship law to ensure Jews of Lithuanian descent and others were able to obtain citizenship. The law reduces bureaucratic obstacles by making it easier for applicants to prove their departure from the country prior to the Second World War.

On August 5, Minister of Culture Sarunas Birutis signed a decree designating the Jewish cemetery in Snipiskes, Vilnius, as a cultural object protected by the state.

In August and September, senior officials and thousands of citizens took part in ceremonies throughout the country to honor the memory of Lithuanian Jews massacred during the Holocaust, marking the 75th anniversary of the event. On August 29, President Dalia Grybauskaite led a remembrance ceremony at a mass murder site in the town of Moletai. In September the Lithuanian Human Rights Center installed memorials known as "stumbling stones" in the memory of 20 Holocaust victims in Vilnius, Kaunas, Siauliai, and Panevezys. On September 23, a monument to the massacred children of the Vilnius ghetto was unveiled in the Brothers Garden of the city's only Jewish school, the Sholom Aleichem Gymnasium. The same day Vice-Speaker of the Parliament Gediminas Kirkilas, Chancellor of the Government Alminas Maciulis and Minister of Defense Juozas Olekas participated in the annual commemoration ceremony at the Paneriai memorial site.

Trafficking in Persons

See the Department of State's *Trafficking in Persons Report* at www.state.gov/j/tip/rls/tiprpt/.

Persons with Disabilities

The law prohibits discrimination against persons with disabilities, although it does not specify the type of disabilities. It prohibits discrimination in housing, transport, telecommunications, judiciary, and cultural and leisure activities. There was no proactive enforcement of these requirements. By September 19, the equal opportunities ombudsman had investigated 27 cases of alleged discrimination based on disability (see section 7.d.).

The law mandates that buildings be accessible to persons with disabilities. According to the most recently available data from the Department of Statistics in 2012, the latest data available, nearly 52 percent of housing complied with this requirement.

In 2012 the European Court of Human Rights ruled that the system for protecting persons with disabilities had serious practical and legal shortcomings. On March 27, parliament amended the civil code and the code of civil procedure to afford persons with mental disabilities greater rights during competency hearings.

Observers criticized the government for its approach to disability rights, including inaccessibility, forced hospitalization, human rights violations in closed institutions and psychiatric wards, restrictions on the right to vote and an inadequate mental health system, which remained among the least reformed areas in the health sector.

The government continued implementation of the National Strategy for Social Integration of People with Disabilities for 2013-19. During the year the Department for the Affairs of the Disabled obligated 13 million euros ($14.3 million) as part of this program.

National/Racial/Ethnic Minorities

The law prohibits discrimination against ethnic or national minorities, but intolerance and societal discrimination persisted. According to 2011 data from the Department of Statistics (the most recent available), approximately 14 percent of the population were members of minority ethnic groups, including Russians, Poles, Belarusians, Ukrainians, Tatars, Karaites, and Jews.

In the first eight months of the year, the Ministry of Interior reported 24 cases of alleged discrimination and incitement of racial, ethnic, religious, or other hatred, compared with 113 cases in 2015. Most of the instances investigated involved the internet. According to a former Vilnius County prosecutor, judges and other law enforcement officials seldom prosecuted these crimes, giving priority to "real-life" crimes with identifiable victims.

The country's national day, February 16, when the state of Lithuania was restored in 1918, and March 11, the date the country declared its independence from the Soviet Union in 1990, continued to be occasions for nationalist manifestations. Marchers chanted the slogan "Lithuania for Lithuanians" on both occasions.

The small Romani community (approximately 3,000 persons) continued to experience discrimination in access to education, housing, health care, employment, and relations with police, although there were no official charges of police abuse. Extreme poverty, illiteracy, and perceived high criminality helped form the negative attitudes of mainstream society that resulted in the social exclusion of Roma. In addition 40 percent of Roma did not know the Lithuanian language. Most adult Roma had identification papers, but a few, although born in the country, were effectively stateless.

In April the Vilnius City Council began a Romani integration plan to move residents from their settlement to state housing in other parts of the city. In the first nine months of the year, the municipality moved six families; however, it could not find housing for three families whose residences were destroyed after being condemned by court order.

The government participated in two Romani commemoration events. On August 2, government representatives laid flowers at the Paneriai Memorial in Vilnius on International Roma Holocaust Remembrance Day. In September the Lithuanian Human Rights Center installed memorials known as "stumbling stones" in the memory of 20 Holocaust victims, including Roma, in Vilnius, Kaunas, Siauliai, and Panevezys.

Representatives of the Polish minority continued raising concerns about education for ethnic minorities in the country. They also complained about a legal requirement that all students, whether native Lithuanian speakers or not, complete a single, uniform Lithuanian language examination at the end of their studies. Restrictions on the use of Polish in street signs and on official documents, particularly passports, remained contentious. Authorities did not take any measures during the year to respond to these concerns. In two court cases on April 6 and June 22, however, Vilnius courts ordered the last names in the birth certificates of two Lithuanian citizens be spelled with the non-Lithuanian letter "W."

Acts of Violence, Discrimination, and Other Abuses Based on Sexual Orientation and Gender Identity

The antidiscrimination laws apply to LGBTI persons. Society's attitude toward LGBTI persons remained largely negative. The few NGOs focusing on LGBTI problems did not face legal impediments. The Lithuanian Gay League (LGL) and Tolerant Youth Association (TYA) continued to promote an inclusive social environment for LGBTI persons.

The latest LGL research found that 54 percent of LGBTI persons surveyed experienced or witnessed instances of hate crimes or hate speech on grounds of sexual orientation or gender identity. Only 13 percent of respondents reported the incidents to law enforcement officials. For instance, in October 2015 the chair of the TYA, Arturas Rudomanskis, submitted a complaint to police, asking them to investigate text messages he received, including death threats. Vilnius County Police refused to initiate an investigation, noting there was not enough evidence that the threats could be carried out. The prosecutor's office, district court, and appeal court all denied Rudomanskis' subsequent appeal regarding the initiation of such an investigation. As of September his complaint was registered with the European Court of Human Rights.

An antipropaganda law enacted in 2009 served as a rationale for limiting LGBTI awareness-raising efforts (see section 2.a.). In July 2015 the European Commission's Directorate General for Communication Networks, Content, and Technology began a formal investigation of a 2014 ruling by the Office of the Inspector of Journalistic Ethics that blocked television broadcast during regular broadcast hours of an LGBTI awareness video produced by the LGL. The office cited the law on protection of minors in blocking the broadcast.

On June 1, the court rejected a Belarusian man's appeal for family reunification with his Lithuanian male spouse. The Migration Department had refused to issue him a residence permit, despite the fact that the law does not specify that reunification based on marriage must be between members of the opposite sex.

On June 18, approximately 2,000 people participated in the Baltic Pride march in Vilnius. Compared with the last march in 2013, municipal authorities showed more responsiveness in providing permits for the event, and there were fewer protesters or attempted disruptions.

HIV and AIDS Social Stigma

The NGO community reported that individuals with HIV/AIDS were often subject to discrimination, including in employment, and treated with fear and aversion.

Other Societal Violence or Discrimination

In the first eight months of the year, the equal opportunities ombudsman investigated 17 cases of age discrimination, including in employment, insurance, loans, and leases. The ombudsman found discrimination in a majority of these cases and made recommendations to the offending institutions.

Section 7. Worker Rights

a. Freedom of Association and the Right to Collective Bargaining

The law provides for the right of workers to form and join independent unions, bargain collectively, and conduct legal strikes. The law prohibits employer discrimination against union organizers and members and requires reinstatement of workers fired for union activity. These provisions also apply to migrant workers.

There were some specific legal limits to these rights. The law prohibits law enforcement and other security-related personnel from collective bargaining or striking, although they may join unions. Labor-code procedures made it difficult for some workers to exercise the right to strike.

The law does not afford workers in essential services, whose right to strike is restricted or prohibited, alternative procedures for impartial and rapid settlement of their claims or a voice in developing such procedures. In the event of a disagreement between management and labor, any such disputes are to be settled by a labor arbitration board formed under the jurisdiction of the district court where the registered office of the enterprise or entity involved in the collective dispute is located.

The government did not enforce the labor laws effectively, although resources, inspections, and remediation were adequate. Penalties ranged from fines to imprisonment and were insufficient to deter violations. According to the International Trade Union Confederation, the judicial system was slow to respond to cases of unfair dismissal, and no employer ever faced the penal sanctions for antiunion discrimination envisaged in the law. No labor courts or judges specialized in labor disputes.

The government generally respected freedom of association. Employers did not always respect collective bargaining rights, and managers often determined wages without regard to union preferences except in large factories with well-organized unions.

b. Prohibition of Forced or Compulsory Labor

The law prohibits all forms of forced or compulsory labor, and the government generally enforced the law effectively. Penalties ranged from a fine to 12 years' imprisonment, which were sufficient to deter violations.

There were instances of forced labor, all of which involved Lithuanian men who were subjected to forced labor abroad. For example, in November, the Klaipeda police commissioner investigated a case where three men were promised well-paid, legal employment in France, but once relocated, they were coerced into stealing merchandise from stores. During the first eight months of the year, authorities opened investigations into 20 alleged cases of trafficking, including six cases of child trafficking.

Also see the Department of State's *Trafficking in Persons Report* at www.state.gov/j/tip/rls/tiprpt/.

c. Prohibition of Child Labor and Minimum Age for Employment

The law sets the minimum age for most employment at 16 but allows the employment of persons as young as 14 for light labor with the written consent of the child's parents and school. The law mandates reduced work hours for children, allowing up to two hours per day or 12 hours per week during the school year and up to seven hours per day or 32 hours per week when school is not in session. The law provides employee under the age of 18 with additional work and leisure guarantees, such as mandating shorter work hours and prohibiting hazardous or overtime work. According to the law, hazardous work is any environment that may cause disease or pose a danger to the employee's life, such as heavy construction or working with industrial chemicals.

The government generally enforced these prohibitions effectively. Resources, inspections, and remediation were adequate to enforce the law. Penalties for violations range from fines of 14 euros ($15.40) to 8,688 euros ($9,560). According to the State Labor Inspectorate, the penalties as imposed by courts were insufficient to deter violations.

The State Labor Inspectorate is responsible for receiving complaints related to employment of persons younger than 18. In the first eight months of the year, the inspectorate identified six instances in which children were working illegally, without work contracts, in the forestry, wholesale, retail, and construction sectors.

d. Discrimination with Respect to Employment and Occupation

The law prohibits employment discrimination on the basis of race, color, sex, religion, language, national origin, social origin, political opinion, age, sexual orientation, disability, and ethnic origin. There was no specific statute concerning HIV-positive status or positive status for other communicable diseases, or gender identity.

The government effectively enforced the law, issuing penalties of 115 to 231 euros ($127 to $254). The penalties were adequate to deter violations.

An amendment to the Law on Equal Opportunities for Women and Men adopted on June 7 stipulates that discrimination on the basis of sex should also cover discrimination on the basis of pregnancy and maternity (childbirth and breastfeeding). In 2014 women occupied 31 percent of senior administrative positions at state institutions. According to the Department of Statistics, the pay gap between men and women in 2015 was 14.5 percent, compared with 13.7 percent in 2013. The Office of the Equal Opportunities Ombudsman (EOO) monitored the implementation of discrimination laws. As of September 1, the ombudsman conducted 127 discrimination investigations, including seven involving discrimination based on social origin, two on religion, 17 on age, one on belief, three on language, four on national origin, one on sexual orientation, and 21 on sex. Of these investigations, 65 were regarding discrimination on the basis of sex or age in employment advertisements. To address this issue, the EOO organized a campaign, "For Competence," aimed at encouraging society to react to discriminatory job advertisements and inform the EOO. As a part of this campaign, the EOO facilitated a training series on equal opportunities for the business community in Vilnius, Klaipeda, Siauliai, Plunge, Mazeikiai, and other towns. Many workers remained unaware of their rights with respect to workplace discrimination.

e. Acceptable Conditions of Work

According to the National Department of Statistics, starting in July the minimum monthly wage was 380 euros ($418). The official "poverty risk level" in 2015 was 256 euros ($282) per month, little changed from 2014. On June 21, parliament adopted amendments to the labor code to take effect in 2017. The new law simplifies dismissal procedures, increases annual maximum overtime hours from 120 to 180, and establishes different categories of work contracts, such as permanent, fixed-term, temporary agency, apprenticeship, project work, job sharing, employee sharing, and seasonal. The existing law provides that the maximum time worked in any seven-day period, including overtime, may not exceed 40 hours for white-collar work and 48 hours for blue-collar work. It allows overtime only in specifically stipulated circumstances, and both overtime and night work must be compensated by at least time and a half the hourly wage. The law gives workers the right to safe and healthy working conditions. The occupational safety and health standards are current and appropriate for the main industries.

The labor laws apply to both national and foreign workers. According to the law, employees can refuse unsafe work without fear of discrimination or retaliation.

The government enforced all these standards effectively across all sectors including the informal economy. According to the law, a fine for first-time offenders ranges from 868 euros ($955) to 2,896 euros ($3,190) and for second-time offenders up to 5,792 euros ($6,370), which was adequate to deter violations. The State Labor Inspectorate, which is responsible for implementing labor laws, had a staff of 140 labor inspectors, which was sufficient to enforce compliance. In the first eight months of the year, the inspectorate received 3,760 complaints, mostly related to labor-contract violations and wages in arrears, and conducted 6,162 inspections at companies and other institutions. The most numerous abuses it found were violations of worker safety and worker contracts. Workers dissatisfied with the results of an investigation can appeal to the court system. The State Labor Inspectorate continued to conduct seminars for managers of companies, local communities, and persons looking for work. The seminars dealt with preventing and combating illegal employment, the administration of labor contracts, and worker's rights.

According to the State Labor Inspectorate, violations of wage, overtime, safety, and health standards occurred primarily in the construction, retail, and manufacturing sectors. The inspectorate received complaints about hazardous conditions from workers in the construction and manufacturing sectors. As of September 1, the State Labor Inspectorate recorded 28 fatal accidents at work and 92 severe work-related injuries, compared with 29 and 98, respectively, in 2015. Most accidents occurred in the transport, construction, processing, and agricultural sectors. To address the problem, the inspectorate continued conducting a series of training seminars for inspectors on technical labor inspection. The law protects the rights of workers to remove themselves from work situations that endanger their health or safety without jeopardy to their continued employment. Workers did not regularly exercise this right. Workers also have the legal right to request compensation for health concerns arising from dangerous working conditions.

www.ingramcontent.com/pod-product-compliance
Lightning Source LLC
Chambersburg PA
CBHW081300250726
48654CB00012B/1667